Eddy FLORENT

The Battle of Normandy

Coordination:
Nathalie LAVIEILLE
Layout:
Anne SABLERY
Translated by:
John LEE

MEMORIAL
CAEN NORMANDIE

EDITIONS OUEST-FRANCE

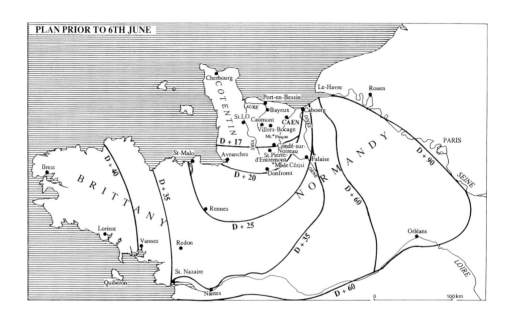

PLAN PRIOR TO 6TH JUNE

SEPTEMBER HORIZON
The Loing between the Seine and the Loire

To reach the Loing by 6th September, where the Seine at Moret and the Loire at Briare flank an easily held 55-mile pass in the event of the German army being still a powerful force, such was the strategic vision of the *Overlord* plan: the battle in Normandy dating from the landing.

In reaching the south bank of the Loire by 6th August and the south bank of the Seine by 6th September, the Allied armies would have a spacious lodgment area in which to assemble possibly some 55 divisions, including the ten or so making their way up the Rhône valley after landing in Provence and due to rejoin the others. The whole set-up to be supplied through the ports of Brittany and the Cotentin.

This logistical springboard would enable the preparation of the decisive operations against Germany: a main thrust on the line Amiens-Maubeuge-Liège-Ruhr, and a secondary thrust on the line Verdun-Metz.

Such was the cautious initial plan when it was decided upon in May 1944. It explains the Battle of Normandy before the unexpected encirclement of the German Seventh Army in the Falaise Pocket. It would be revised, turned upside down, discussed, then sped up after the situation suddenly took a favourable turn with the enemy's general order to withdraw. In the last days of August 1944, it was subjected to a rapid reorganization, making the Allied forces, until then facing eastwards, wheel round veering north, beyond the Seine. There would be no further check until they had raced to the German border; and then either being unable to keep up with the advance because of a fuel shortage, or because the German army recovered in the Vosges or behind the Siegfried line.

D-Day Chiefs of Staff: standing, General Omar Bradley, Admiral Bertram Ramsay, Air-Chief Marshall Trafford Leigh-Mallory, Lieutenant-General Walter B. Smith; seated: Air-Chief Marshall Arthur Tedder, General Dwight D. Eisenhower, General Bernard Law Montgomery.

100 DAYS
for a springboard on the German frontier

Midnight on 6th June 1944: 156,205 American, British, Canadian and French soldiers held eight sites, along a 50 mile front on the Normandy coastline, between Amfreville-sur-Orne in the east and Sainte-Mère-Eglise in the west, at a cost of 10,800 casualties, a third of whom were killed.

132,715 of these troops had landed from the sea, 23,490 others had been dropped from the air. The seaborne had been shipped in 4,126 vessels with 1,213 warships in support, in 47 convoys manned by 96,000 sailors. The airborne had jumped from some 1,900 aircraft (883 for the two American paratroop divisions, a thousand including 368 gliders for the British pa-

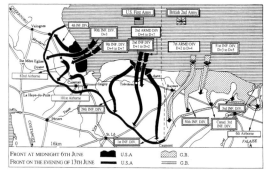

FRONT AT MIDNIGHT 6TH JUNE ▬▬ U.S.A ▨▨ G.B.
FRONT ON THE EVENING OF 13TH JUNE ▬▬ U.S.A ══ G.B.

ratroop division), having taken off from 22 airfields. The entire liberating forces had received overhead protection with 10,753 sorties.

The first of the hundred days of the Battle of Normandy was one of grave disappointments that would weigh heavily on the timetable and the progress of a campaign designed to obtain, as a priority, the ports and the flat ground:
- in the east, neither Cabourg nor Troarn, which were to have offered the protective obstacle of the Dives and its hills, had fallen;

- in the south, Caen, which, from the evening of 6th June, was to have opened the gateway to the plain suitable for the construction of airfields, was ruled out by a German reaction, and a successful one, improvised on the evening of 6th June. Falaise, where Montgomery had intended to push a powerful armoured force on the evening of *D-Day*, had not been attained;
- in the south-west, the Bayeux-Isigny road, the lifeline between the Commonwealth forces which had come ashore in the east and the American forces which had landed in the west, had not been cut off;
- in the west, Port-en-Bessin, at the head of the oil pipe to be rolled out towards the front, had not been liberated;
- in the north-west, the Merderet, which had to be crossed in order to cut off the Cotentin peninsula, had not been crossed;
- neither Pont-l'Abbé nor Quinéville, the launch pad for the vital thrust towards Cherbourg, were in American hands;
- the five beaches and the three dropping zones had not been linked up, and would not be until 12th June.

Some of the *D-Day* objectives would not be achieved until 16th August (Falaise), 17th August (Troarn), 21st August (Cabourg).

By that time, 2,052,299 Allies (1,229,659 under American command, 829,640 under British command), under the supreme command of General Eisenhower, had brought the Battle of Normandy to its conclusion. With casualties lighter than anticipated, 209,672 victims, including 36,976 killed, 153,475 wounded, 19,221 missing.

Coming from the west, 17 divisions (including 4 armoured and 1 parachute), and 8 brigades commanded by General Montgomery, 23 divisions (including 6 armoured and 2 parachute), under General Bradley, now turned towards the heart of Germany.

On the other side, they were confronted with 42 German infantry and 11 armoured divisions that would withdraw, from 16th August, to the Scheldt, to the Rhine, to the Vosges.

And while Luxemburg and the greater part of Belgium were liberated in the meantime, the assault on the entrenched camp of Le Havre, on 12th September, marked the hundredth and final day of the Battle of Normandy, on the very eve of the historic crossing of the German border, 10 miles south of Aachen.

1 - 20,000 vehicles landed on 6th June at a cost of 291 barges lost.
2 - On 6th June, 18 German divisions including the 12th SS (here) mustered from the Aure, were on the spot between the Seine and Loire rivers.

NUMBER ONE REQUIREMENT: ports and airfields

Before gathering the forces that would rush to Germany, the Chiefs of Staff had two priorities;
- ports were required; these were in Brittany;
- airstrips were needed; the necessary space for them was in the plains between Caen and Falaise.

For this reason, in the spring of 44, Montgomery decided upon the following strategy;
- in the west, for U.S. First Army under General Bradley, to seize Cherbourg, Avranches, Rennes and to cut Brittany off at the Quiberon peninsula, precisely where the landing had been initially envisaged;
- in the east, for British Second Army under General Dempsey, to pivot around Caen to constitute a powerful front in the region of Falaise.

To understand the ups and downs of a campaign which although failing to meet the scheduled timetable yet turned out shorter than anticipated, it is necessary to keep well in mind the two reflexes of the Allied strategy: Brittany in the west, Falaise to the south.

British Second Army (General Dempsey, back to camera) and the US First Army (General Bradley) remained under orders from General Montgomery (facing the map) until 31st July.

CHERBOURG: neither D + 8, nor D + 15 but D + 20

Eisenhower, commanding the entire land, sea and air forces, and Montgomery, commanding the entire land forces, had set out the timetable for the first common objectives, from the spring of 1944: first Caen, Bayeux and the Saint-Lô road; then the Falaise road and the capture of Cherbourg.

The hazards of the battle meant that the second objective, Bayeux, was achieved first (on the morning of 7th June), followed by the fifth objective: Cherbourg, originally anticipated for D + 8, "granted", at Bradley's request, on D + 15, and finally attained on D + 20.

4th American Infantry, which had landed at Utah, set off towards Montebourg on 7th June, whilst the two American parachute divisions seized Carentan (101st Airborne) on the 12th, and Saint-Sauveur-le-Vicomte (82nd Airborne) on 16th June.

With the capture of Isigny (9th) and Caumont (12th and 13th) secured by American units that had come ashore at Omaha, the five beachheads were linked up into a single lodgement.

The Americans of General Collins' VII Corps cut off the Cotentin peninsula on the 18th at Barneville, and then turned northwards with 9th Infantry on the western flank, 79th Infantry in the middle, and 4th Infantry to the east. Cherbourg was liberated on the 26th, Bradley covered the entire northern coast on the 27th. Henceforth, Cherbourg was ready to take in 15,000 tons per day.

ALLIED LOSSES BY 30th JUNE
61,732 soldiers including 8,469 killed (3,356 among the Anglo-Canadian forces, 5,113 among the Americans), 42,353 wounded, 10,910 missing.
Allied pilots flew 163,403 sorties, including maritime and long-distance operations, at a cost of 1,508 machines lost and 6,253 airmen killed or missing.

1 - The US 79th Infantry Division (General Wyche) captured 36,006 prisoners during the assault on Cherbourg.
2 - The first convoy of equipment arriving from England entered Cherbourg harbour on 13th July, the first four Liberty ships on the 16th. The first US troops landed on 26th July.

CAEN
at a cost of 34 days of bloodshed: 9th July

Late in the afternoon of D-Day, mishaps encountered by 3rd British Infantry on the beach at Hermanville on the morning of 6th June, together with delays caused by the bloody battles to reduce the earthworks buried in the first slopes rising towards Caen, brought to a halt the frontal advance on the city which they had hoped to launch that same evening; 21st Panzer, after having threatened the link-up of the beachheads at Sword and Juno, only just to cling onto Lebisey wood, on the outskirts of Caen. With the arrival, in spite of the bombs, of 3 other German armoured divisions - 12th SS, 2nd Panzer, Panzer Lehr -, a tough shield now hindered the initial plans. Therefore Montgomery resolved on an improvised strategy of envelopment:

- a first attempt to capture Caen from the southwest failed: the Desert Rats (7th British Armoured) and 50th British Infantry, who had hoped to take the city in a scything movement from Tilly-sur-Seulles to Livry and Villers-Bocage on 12th and 13th June, lost 25 tanks, 14 armoured cars and 14 half-tracks under Hill 213 defended by 2nd Panzer and the Panzer Lehr. So they turned back;

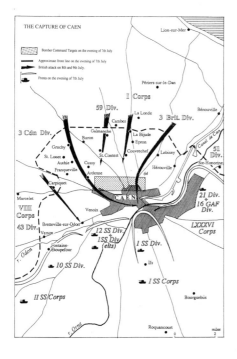

The Panzer Lehr came to reinforce 12th SS Panzer and 21st Panzer taking up a position on 8th June south of Tilly-sur-Seulles, in the hope of throwing the British back into the sea.

- **a second attempt to seize Caen in a pincer movement failed:** Operation *Epsom*, launched on 25th June, aborted on 1st July, was intended to take British VIII Corps onto the strategic high ground at Bourguébus, by crossing the Odon and Orne rivers to the west of Caen, in order to link up, on the far side of the Caen-Cagny road, with 51st Highland who were to come from the north from the beachhead of the paratroops of 6th Airborne, (60,000 men, 500 naval guns). At high cost: 4,020 killed and wounded. For a consolation prize: eight panzer divisions had streamed across to the Caen-Caumont front, thus diverting them from the projected powerful counter-offensive intended to throw the Allies back into the sea;

- **a third, frontal, attempt only managed to liberate certain sectors of the left bank:** Operation *Charnwood*, led by 115,000 men (3rd British Infantry, 51st Highland, 3rd Canadian Infantry), and supported by 460 bombers dropping over 2,600 tons of 1000 and 500 pound bombs on the northern quarters of Caen, cost 80 tanks and 3,500 men. On 9th July, the Canadians entered a city 80% destroyed, down to less than 4,000 inhabitants. They would be harassed for nearly a month by the shells of 12th SS, on the high ground at Vaucelles, blocking the road to Falaise.

In a two-day battle for Caen, Canadian 3rd Division alone lost 1,194 men including 330 killed.

THREE THRUSTS FAIL to break out towards Falaise

The capture of Caen solved nothing. The Germans reorganised at the access points astride the Falaise road, well aware of the importance of the plains that they were denying.

Montgomery was therefore obliged to launch thrust after thrust, confident that each one would be decisive. In vain:

- **Operation *Jupiter:*** on 10th and 11th July, to break out towards Falaise via the west of Caen. Objective: to reach passages upstream of the Orne by seizing Hill 112, south-west of Maltot, already fought over during Operation *Epsom.* Supported by 40,000 shells, 43rd Wessex took the hill on 10th July. 9th and 10th SS regained it on the 11th, lost it again on the 12th, attempted to reconquer it the same day. The British had lost 2,000 of their men. The hill remained uncertain. A failure.

- **Operation *Greenline*:** From 15th to 17th July, to break out towards Falaise, again via the west of Caen. Objective: to seize Hill 113 in order to prepare the advance on Aunay or Thury-Harcourt as the opportunity should arise; simultaneously, to secure the region around Noyers so as to prepare to exploit towards the high ground north-east of Villers-Bocage. 15th Scottish, 49th West Riding, 53rd Welsh and 59th Staffordshires lost over 3,500 men in ten days in the attempt. A failure.

- **Operation *Goodwood:*** on 18th July, to break out towards Falaise, this time outflanking Caen on the east. Objective: to seize all Orne crossings, from Caen to Falaise. Three British armoured divisions - 75,000 men, 1,300 tanks, 750 guns - who had left the beachhead at Bénouville, supported by 2,500 bombers dropping 8,000 tons of bombs in three hours, hoped to cross the Caen-Falaise road and reach the banks of the Laize, from Laize to Bretteville. But they came to a halt before Bourguébus, having lost 400 tanks and sustained 5,537 casualties in two days.

On 13th June alone, at Villers-Bocage, Panzer Lehr, who had lost 5 tanks and 130 vehicles on their way to the front, lost another 6 Tiger tanks and several Mark IVs.

By 19th July, total British losses since D-Day had risen to 34,700 men (including 6,010 killed) and American losses had reached 62,028 (including 10,641 killed).

In order to take Hill 112 on the Caen-Aunay road, 43rd Wessex posted 2,000 casualties on 10th and 11th July.

SAINT-LÔ, the capital of the ruins, for start point: 18th July

Having seized La Haye-du-Puits on 8th July, and got beyond Sainteny on the 15th, at great cost in the course of the unexpected battles of the hedgerows (2,300 men lost in 10 days by 4th Infantry; almost 5,000 in 12 days for 83rd Infantry; 3,000 men for 30th Infantry; roughly 2,500 men for 9th Infantry), General Bradley realigned two of his four corps to the north of the line Lessay-Périers-Saint-Lô across the peninsula in preparation for escaping the confining Cotentin in order to gain breathing space before breaking out into Brittany.

It nevertheless remained to take Saint-Lô, soon known as "the Cassino of the north".

This task was entrusted to 2nd Infantry (which on 11th July was to occupy the terrible Hill 192 above Saint-Georges-d'Elle, overlooking the firing line, and pounded so heavily by the artillery that an American officer described it as looking like "a white moth-eaten woollen

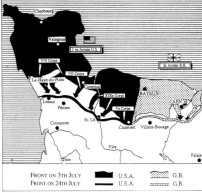

blanket"); a task also allocated to 35th Infantry (that was to crush, on 15th July, the defences on Hill 122 where the slightest farm was transformed into a redoubt in the hands of General Meindl's three *Kampfgruppen* and General Schimpf's 3rd parachute division).

A task assigned more particularly to 29th Infantry: General Gerhardt's soldiers entered, on 18th July, **thirty days behind schedule**, in a city that - ravaged by "a deluge of iron and fire", "so badly hit by the first bombardment of 6th June that left 800 dead that many of the people of Saint-Lô did not believe a return of the bombers possible" - offered them scenes "that could be described only by Dante".

The Americans now held what an officer of 35th Infantry would call "the gate to the interior of France".

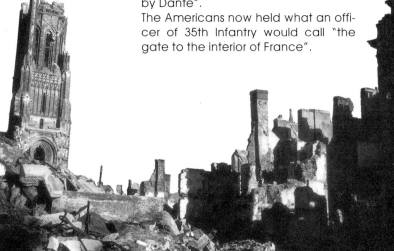

A week of fighting for Saint-Lô, where 800 civilians were killed under the bombs on 7th June, one of many daily bombing raids against the town intended to make it a choke-point to hinder the arrival of enemy reinforcements.

TARGET BRITTANY
Bradley breaks out at Avranches

To occupy Brittany, a launch pad for the large-scale eastward dash, such was the aim of Operation *Cobra*, launched on 25th July to exit the Cotentin where the main portion of the American forces had so far been contained from Saint-Lô to Lessay.

Preceded by 1,579 bombers and 400 fighter-bombers pouring 5,000 incendiary bombs per square kilometer over a 12 km² area between Saint-Gilles, Marigny and Hébecrévon, three American infantry divisions, followed by four armoured divisions, cut the German armour to pieces.

Avranches fell on 30th July, Rostrenen and Rennes were liberated on 4th August, Lorient and Brest were reached on 7th August, during which time a new American army, commanded by a commander who had entered the history of the Second World War in North Africa and Sicily - General Patton - undertook a colossal turning movement in direction of Le Mans. Speaking of his objectives at Brest, Saint-Nazaire, Orléans and Le Mans, and with his eye on Alençon, the commander of Third Army cried, "For the first time in the history of war, an army is attacking in all four directions at once!"

A German general warned his men: "The repercussions of any breakout into Brittany will be incalculable!"

The Allies in Normandy on 1st August 1944			
21st Army Group: US	First Army	Gen Hodges	12 divs.
	Second Army	Gen Hodges	9 divs.
21st Army Group: UK	British Second Army	Gen Dempsey	6 divs.
	Canadian First Army	Gen Crérar	10 divs.

Hitler's mistake at Mortain exposes German Seventh Army to encirclement

Twelve American divisions surged, "bumper to bumper", along the gully from Avranches to Pontaubault, a frail umbilical cord, and headed off either towards Brittany or the Loire, or again towards the Maine. Hitler felt the wind of disaster and dreamed of strangling this wave of armour at its trouble spot. The Fuehrer devised a thrust to the Mont-Saint-Michel, by gathering units already allocated to holding the front facing Caen. This risky seesaw game was contested by his generals; to weaken the front before Montgomery in order to attack Bradley was possibly to help Montgomery achieve his strategic obsession, namely the thrust down to Falaise.

It was a risk Hitler nevertheless took; Operation *Luttich*, launched before dawn on 7th August, with 3 armoured divisions down to 145 tanks and 32 assault guns, aimed at penning the Americans back in the Cherbourg peninsula whilst stretching out a hand to the German forces in Brittany. Ignoring the German counter-offensive and leaving General Hodges' First Army, duly informed, if not reassured by the decoding of enemy messages obtained by the Enigma / ULTRA machine, to deal with it, four American corps under General Patton swung off to the Atlantic coast and the Loire while closing north behind German Seventh Army, henceforth caught in the trap partly of its own making. An exultant Bradley exclaimed: "This is an opportunity that comes to a commander not more than once a century! We are about to destroy an entire German army!"

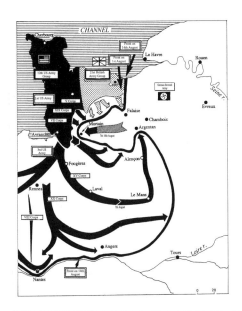

Mortain, "liberated" on 3rd August by US 1st Inf, encircled on the 7th by 2nd and 17th SS, and finally cleared on 12th August by US 30th Inf.

Hitler's miscalculation in precipitating the German forces of Normandy into the trap at Mortain upset the initial Allied strategy; the Americans reduced the effort towards the Loire,

MONTGOMERY, moves down from the north, towards Falaise. PATTON moves up from the south, towards Argentan

along a line Bretteville-Cintheaux-Saint Aignan de Cramesnil. Later, on 10th August, Canadian 4th Armoured and Polish 1st Armoured consolidated this effort, failing however to get beyond Soignolles, Estrées and Quesnay wood ravaged by bombs. Falaise was another 5 miles away;

preferring to sweep round towards Alençon; the Commonwealth forces, at the southern exits from Caen, put off plans to attack towards the Seine in favour of "going all out" (*Totalize*) on the Falaise road with the aim of linking up behind the German Seventh Army to cut off its escape route to the Seine;

- **Operation *Bluecoat***, the breakout from the hedgerow country by British XII and XXX Corps, in a south-easterly

- **Operation *Tractable*** on 14th August (the day Leclerc's 2nd Armoured, having liberated Alençon on the 12th and Ecouché on the 13th, were approaching Argentan and the Americans were at Bourg-Saint-Léonard) abandoned the head-on thrust in fa-

direction through Caumont-Jurques-Mont Pinçon (captured on 7th August), was the start of the envelopment of the German Seventh Army on its north-western flank;

- **Operation *Totalize***, on 8th August, entrusted to the three Canadian divisions and to the Polish 1st Armoured, under General Maczek, was intended to reach Falaise that same evening with a directly frontal assault. At first, Canadian 2nd Infantry and the 51st Highlanders were stopped by 12th SS Panzer

vour of a manoeuvre towards Trun. Canadian 4th Armoured and Polish 1st Armoured were given orders to threaten Falaise from the north-east, by crossing the Laizon whilst Canadian 2nd Infantry, British 53rd Infantry and British 59th Infantry attacked the town from the north-west. Falaise, a dead town, fell into the hands of the Canadians of 2nd Infantry under General Foulkes on 16th August, with not a soul among the ruins to welcome their liberators.

1 - British 11th Armoured enters Saint-Martin-des-Besaces on 31st July, day 2 of Operation *Bluecoat*.
2 - Two days fighting for May-sur-Orne, finally liberated by the Mont-Royal Fusiliers on 8th August.
3 - Falaise, a D-Day target that fell on 16th, 17th and 18th August to the Canadian 2nd Division.

THE RING IS CLOSED on the evening of 19th August at Chambois

Crossing the Argentan road at Bourg-Saint-Léonard and advancing through Gouffern forest, the American 90th Infantry Division and particularly the 359th Infantry Regiment, entered Chambois from the south, where roads from all four points of the compass meet; there they shook hands with the Poles of the 10th Dragoons from General Maczek's division, who had come down from the high ground to the north-east, near the tormented sector of Mont Ormel.

The ring was closed, all the more so since 2 miles further west, the South Alberta Regiment's C Squadron led by Major D.V. Currie held the northern exit at Saint-Lambert-sur-Dives firmly shut.

Between these two positions, "the appalling scramble to get out" (Patton) saw crumble, over a period of three days, the remnants of the harassed German army, sometimes starving, often thirsty, seeking to escape through "death corridor" (Moissy ford, on the Dives) rising up to Mont Ormel, altitude 262 m, where two Polish tank regiments were holding out after crossing the Dives at Jort. The "cauldron", which entered the history books under the name of "Falaise", although the fighting actually took place in the Dives basin, was to bubble away until the morning of 22nd August; Eisenhower later described it as "one of the greatest 'killing grounds' of any of the war areas", given the density of the battle and the number of days fighting. While some German generals, among whom some of those who were closest to Hitler, would talk of "Das Stalingrad der Normandie".

Enclosed in the ring of fire and steel formed by 11 Allied divisions exultant that victory was at hand - one Polish division to the north, three Canadian divisions to the north-east and north-west, four British divisions to the west, two American divisions to the south-west, one French division (2nd Armoured) to the south-east, the German units, squeezing out "like toothpaste out of a tube", along a line Putanges-Nécy-Bailleul-Chambois, sought to break loose, under rocketfire from the Typhoons, furrowing the sky and shells converging from all directions on the hollow depression of the Dives; and made a headlong rush - "a real anthill", one Polish staff officer called it - for Coudehard, with access to the Vimoutiers road, where the remnants of two SS divisions rushed from outside the pocket. Left to their own devices on the cone of Mont Ormel, the Polish regiments played out so as to fire in all directions:

"Acting as a cork to keep the Germans enclosed as in a bottle" (Montgomery), after many critical hours cut off from the main body of Canadian II Corps, they would leave eleven burnt out Shermans on the hill. Since General Maczek's division was committed to the battle of Normandy, this division, made up of volunteers from occupied France, Europe under the German heel, the U.S., Canada and Great Britain - the most highly motivated unit of the entire Allied army, and the one that took the greatest risks over the entire campaign in the western theatre of operations - in the space of twelve days lost 10% of its

Previous page:
14th August on the Caen-Falaise road; the Americans bombarding the Canadians. A mistake...

18

men with 325 including 21 officers killed, 1,002 including 35 officers wounded, and 114 missing.

For Bradley, "more than 70,000 demoralised Germans were killed or captured in this pocket. The bulk of 19 German divisions was ground to pieces in the pocket". For Martin Blumenson, official historian of the United States army, "from 20,000 to 40,000 Germans escaped from the Falaise Gap". For German General Eberbach, "the number of Germans who escaped from encirclement after the closing of the pocket can be estimated at 20,000, that of men killed during the battle from 10th to 22th August, at 30,000". For General Speidel, Army Group B Chief of Staff, "out of 6 armoured divisions, barely 100 tanks returned". For Field-Marshal Model, "five decimated divisions made it back to Germany. The remains of 11 infantry divisions went to reconstituting 4 units, each with a handful of artillery guns and other small equipment. What was left of 11 tank divisions when they were renewed in men and material, amounted to 11 regiments each with 5 to 6 tanks and a few artillery batteries."

On 19th August, when the fighting to escape encirclement had not yet begun, Montgomery, counting German losses since 6th June, mentions "20 commanders killed or captured, 2 army commanders wounded, 2 supreme commanders dismissed (von Rundstedt, then von Kluge, replaced by Model after 16th August), 40 divisions eliminated or savagely mauled, at least 200,000 enemy losses, over 3,000 guns captured and destroyed, over 1,000 tanks destroyed".

The Army Group B diary (German Seventh Army and German Fifteenth Army, the "Pas-de-Calais"), reckoned that the 6 or 7 armoured divisions that managed to filter out of the Pocket numbered less than 2,000 men, 62 tanks and 26 pieces of artillery.

"Even though the battle of the Falaise-Argentan pocket did not accomplish the utter annihilation of the German armies in Normandy, they were broken as an effective fighting force, and our way across France was opened", concluded Eisenhower.

"It is the beginning of the end of the war!" proclaimed Montgomery, then commanding the 16 divisions of 21st Army.

"The enemy had to escape for 340 miles, from Argentan to the German border", exulted Bradley, then commanding the 21 divisions of the American army group.

Not forgetting three German divisions trapped in Brittany, and an infantry division tied down in the Channel Islands.

At the entrance to Saint-Lambert-sur-Dives on 19th August, Major Currie (left) closes the western flank of the pocket at Chambois.

APPROACHING THE PARIS AREA the "long envelopment"

The whole carefully planned operational strategy - the so-called *Post-Overlord* plan - had been upset; everything was going well, and the Allies were driving eastward.

From 15th August, in view of the favourable developments, American XV Corps, which had helped to press the Falaise Pocket on its southern flank by reaching the Argentan road at Bourg-Saint-Léonard, and even pushing on to Nonant-le-Pin, was detailed to drive on at full speed to the River Eure at Nogent-le-Roi, there to effect first a turning movement to the north, with their sights on Posny-sur-Seine and Mantes, then to make a ninety degree turn, to the left, **westwards**, towards Louviers and maybe Elbeuf, so as to catch up with the units that had eluded them at Mont Ormel, before they crossed the Seine; this was the "long envelopment".

While 79th Infantry (the division that had liberated Cherbourg and held the southern flank of the Falaise Pocket below Argentan) crossed the river, both at Méricourt during the **same night** of 19th August when their comrades-at-arms of 90th Infantry were fighting in Chambois, and at Rosny on the 20th (the same day as the battle for Mont Ormel was engaged), the tanks of 5th Armoured rolled across the plain overlooking Vernon and Gaillon. Patton who had meanwhile seized Dreux, Chartres and Orléans on the 16th, crossed the Seine on the 23rd at Tilly (north of Melun) and Fontainebleau, reached the River Loing

In five nights of ferrying men across the Seine, 300,000 Germans and 25,000 vehicles eluded the Allies.

at Montargis that same day, entering Melun and Troyes on the 25th, the day of the liberation of Paris.

The planned *Overlord* objectives for D + 90 (i.e. 6th September) were achieved twelve days prior to that date. Any backlog had been caught up. But the long envelopment had to be stopped in its tracks within sight of Louviers; it being necessary to make room for British Second Army marching towards crossing points at Vernon and Saint-Pierre-du-Vauvray.

1 - From 20th August, eight floating Bailey bridges (here General Patton) and three pontoons on pneumatic boats, including four in tidal waters, were thrown across the Seine.
2 - Crossing the Seine at Vernon, on 25th and 26th August, by 43rd Wessex, the starting signal for the race to Belgium.

OPERATION *PADDLE* : heading due north via the Seine and the Somme

The left flank of the Allied bridgehead, which for seventy days had courageously protected the bridgehead, well out of the media limelight, whilst the decisive battle was being fought in the west, then the centre, was on the move. Direction: the Seine. And beyond; the Somme where a possible enemy reorganisation was to be feared, and the plains of Picardy and Flanders to put an end to the threat of V1 and V2 rockets hammering the south-east of Britain.

D-Day: 17th August.

Canadian First Army under General Crerar, swung round towards the Seine, from the estuary to Pont-l'Arche;
- British I Corps under General Crocker, entrusted the Red Berets, 6th Airborne under General Gale, the Belgians of the brigade commanded by Lieutenant-Colonel Piron, and the Dutch led by Lieutenant-Colonel Ruyter Van Steveninck, with liberating the "côte fleurie" from Sollenelles to Honfleur, to cross the Touques at Pont-l'Evêque, and the Risle at Pont-Audemer, which they reached on 25th August;
- Canadian II Corps under General Simonds, flushed with victory at Falaise, was to press on to Elbeuf (26th August) after freeing Orbec, Bernay and Brionne.
- **British Second Army** under General Dempsey, would order 43rd Wessex, on its right, to cross the river at Vernon (25th August) and on its left, 15th Scottish, to cross the Seine at Saint-Pierre-du-Vauvray (27th August). The race to Belgium was on, with Brussels and Antwerp the objectives given to each of the corps spearheaded by these divisions.

17th August: the left flank of Operation *Paddle*, the march to the Seine estuary, is entrusted to the Belgians and Luxemburgers of the Piron brigade.

THE SURPRISE OF THE CAMPAIGN:
Paris liberated
42 days early

"My dear general, it is always fine for a leader to be optimistic. I applaud your enthusiasm, but liberate Paris by Christmas and none of us can ask for more!" Churchill had told Eisenhower, when the supreme commander, in the preceding spring, had presented him with plans he judged to "paint too rosy a picture"; Paris, indeed, had been scheduled for liberation some time after 6th October, without any precise date being fixed.

But the destruction of the German army in Normandy was able to release forces hitherto assigned to more urgent strategic missions; the Leclerc division, which had notched up Alençon, the Perche, Argentan, the guard at Mont Ormel, and spurred on by General de Gaulle's resolute stand with the Allied authorities, was detached from XV Corps after 22nd August, and raced to the capital, in the

hands of the Resistance, to enter the city alongside American 4th Infantry Division (which had landed at Utah on D-Day), with all the church bells ringing, on the evening of 24th August.

1 - The liberation of Paris took a toll of 901 Free French and 581 civilians killed, 3,467 Free French and 2,012 civilians wounded, and 223 Free French captured.
2 - At the entrance to Rambouillet, General Leclerc plans the liberation of Paris on 23rd August.

ON DAY 100, a bloodstained final note: Le Havre

Having liberated Rouen on 30th August and taken their revenge at Dieppe on 2nd September, the Canadians continued their advance to Flanders which they had not been expecting to cross so soon. On their left, however, the Englishmen of 49th Division and Highlanders of 51st Division had the thankless task of laying a twelve-day siege on the entrenched camp of Le Havre - 400 works, 77,000 mines, 115 guns - in which 11,000 Germans had taken refuge and which housed 40,000 civilians out of the 170,000 of four years before.

After requesting the enemy to surrender the fortress without a fight, General Crocker, commanding British I Corps, had hoped to avoid making an assault by resorting to seven heavy bomber raids. On 5th September alone, 348 Lancasters, Stirlings and Mosquitoes flew over in six waves, dropping 1,812 tons of explosive bombs and 30,000 incendiary bombs in two hours. Over 2,000 civilian victims, maybe 2,600 or even 3,000, died during this unjustified and badly targeted raid still unexplained fifty years on. 85% of a city had been razed for just 9 Germans killed. Late in the afternoon of 10th September, after a final attempt at negotiations between the two camps, the assault was given by the two infantry divisions, reinforced by two armoured brigades, using the same engines as on 6th June; Crabs, Crocodiles, Avres, etc. Offshore, the Royal Navy, including the battleship *Warspite*, provided support for this operation code-named Astonia.

In an engagement lasting 36 hours, the British and Scottish, who had lost 30 men, infiltrated the streets of Le Havre to be welcomed with no embraces under the only French flags required to celebrate the liberation... at half-mast!

2 MILLION ALLIED SOLDIERS IN NORMANDY

In 87 days of the campaign, over 2 million men, over 438,000 vehicles and over 3 million tons of equipment and supplies were landed in Normandy.

	Commonwealth	Americans	Total
Men	829,640	1,222,659	2,052,299
Vehicles	202,789	235,682	438,491
Equipment (tons)	1,245,625	1,852,634	3,098,259

438,386 FIGHTING MEN KILLED OR WOUNDED ON BOTH SIDES between 6th June and 29th August				
	Killed	Wounded	Missing	Total
21st Army Group (British, Canadian Polish, Belgian, Dutch)	16,138	58,594	9,093	83,825
12th Army Group American (inc. Leclerc's French 2nd Arm'd)	20,838	94,881	10,128	125,847
Royal Air Force	8,178		included in losses	8,178
US Air Force	8,536		"	
Allied losses (in preparatory ops)	12,000		"	12,000
German Army	200,000		200,000 prisoners	400,000 losses

Sources : Supreme Command Report (Pogue USA). Victory in the West (Ellis. G.-B.)

Le Havre in ruins.

THE RIGHT FLANK OF *OVERLORD* the landing in Provence. A continuous front from Switzerland to the Scheldt

The very day the Battle of Normandy came to an end, on 12th September, the spearhead troops of *Overlord* - an element of Leclerc's 2nd Armoured Division - joined hands with the spearhead of *Anvil* which landed in Provence on 15th August: 6 French divisions and 3 American divisions.

The landing in Provence, which Eisenhower wanted on 6th June, to coincide with the Normandy landing, but which Montgomery refused on the pretext of allocating men and equipment to the success of the Normandy landing, was designed to secure the right flank of the Allied force arriving from the west, by targetting the threshold of Burgundy, a common objective for both landings. The link up took place on 12th September between Dijon and Chatillon-sur-Seine.

79,000 Germans captured during operations along the Mediterranean coasts and in the Rhône valley, with 19,000 more hemmed in between the Rhône valley, the Loire and the Atlantic, not forgetting the three German divisions trapped in Brittany and the unusable infantry division in the Channel Islands, thus posed no further threat to the right flank - an unprotected stretch of 650 miles from the Atlantic to the Vosges - menacing the armies coming out of Normandy.

And, during the single month of September, Marseilles would discharge 326,813 tons of goods compared with 314,431 for Cherbourg. And soon more than Antwerp. The broad front, from Switzerland to the Scheldt, as Eisenhower had wished, took shape on 13th September. And made it pos-

15th August 1944: the US 45th Division lands at La Nartelle.

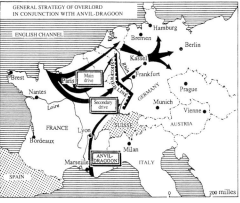

GENERAL STRATEGY OF OVERLORD
IN CONJUNCTION WITH ANVIL-DRAGOON

sible to reinforce with 16 divisions from southern France the application of the directive which had served as the framework of the Normandy campaign: "to enter the continent of Europe and (...) undertake operations aimed at the heart of Germany and the destruction of her armed forces". Eisenhower could now view this whole great enterprise stretching from Marseilles to the lower Rhine as one single theatre of operations.

Normand-Provence in Burgundy: 12th September. An element of 12th Cuirassiers (Captain Gaudet) who landed in Normandy, arrives at Nod-sur-Seine to shake hands with the vanguard of the 1st DFL (Captain Guérard) who landed in Provence.

27

NORMANDY RAVAGED

421 towns and villages housing 78% of the Norman population were hit, 385,000 buildings were completely destroyed or seriously damaged. 42,000 hectares of agricultural land (including 7,900 in the lower Seine area and 60 in the Eure) had been turned into minefields. All bridges and other constructive works had been wiped out; Normandy was the most ravaged province of France. The Manche numbered 15,000 dead, 137,000 total disaster victims, 143,000 partial victims; 390 towns out of 647 were more or less badly affected with 60,000 buildings damaged or destroyed, including 10,000 razed; 30,000 farms out of 50,000 had suffered from the battle; 68 religious structures in the district of Coutances were totally destroyed, 157 would long remain unusable. Valognes, which numbered over 300 dead, had lost 988 buildings; 3,946 of its 4,989 residents were victims. In Cherbourg, bombed 65 times, no more than 1,805 habitations remained out of 4,954. In Le Mesnil-Rouxelin, after 31 days on the front line, a single house was left standing out of 81. Mortain registered over half of its houses (394) as unusable; 1,111 of its

"Massacres, suffering and destruction: Normandy endured these more than any other province. However nothing changed their resolution to help the Allies in reconquering lost freedoms" (Marcel Baudot).

1,726 residents were victims. As for Saint-Lô...

For the department of the Calvados alone, the worst hit places went from Tilly-la-Campagne (96%) to Troarn (65%), with, in between, Villers-Bo-cage (88%), Epron (81%), Lisieux (75%), Vire (73%), Caen (73% with 400 houses intact out of 18,000 in 1944), Falaise (69%).

The lower Seine was no better off: 17,000 out of 19,000 buildings were destroyed or damaged in Le Havre, 18,000 out of 23,000 buildings of Rouen were demolished or unusable, Sotteville suffered 3,000 smashed houses. And Dieppe 850.

Reconstruction would take at least ten years, the figure quoted for the Calvados.

100,000 Normans were requisitio-ned, on the spot, for the German army. 42,139 labourers were trans-ferred to Germany. Out of 3,095 de-portees, 1,506 died in the concen-tration camps. 2,483 Normans belonging to the 101 referenced networks and maquis bringing toge-ther 22,051 active resistants on the eve of the landing were executed or killed in action: 1,243 in the lower Seine, 262 in the Calvados, 481 in the Orne, 242 in the Eure, 255 in the Manche.

No definite figure could ever be to be put on the civilians killed in the five departments of Normandy; figures range from 15,000 to 20,000, maybe as high as 35,000.

FRANCE, LUXEMBURG, BELGIUM: liberated earlier than expected

Twenty days after the liberation of Paris, the Allies reached the frontier of the Reich. In the *Overlord* planners' initial calculations, the line of the Somme was not expected to be crossed before D + 120, i.e. 6th October. However, Brussels (3rd September), Antwerp (4th September), Liège (8th September), for instance, had been liberated long before then.

Aachen, which was expected to fall only on D + 332 (2nd May 1945) after "the establishment of a prudent basis on the Seine and a series of actions intended to push the enemy back to the German frontier" was neverthe-less approached on 14th September, and occupied on 21st October. Indeed, the "pockets" along the Channel and the Atlantic - Boulogne, Calais, Dunkirk on the one hand; Lorient, Quiberon, Saint-Nazaire, La Pallice-La Rochelle, Royan, Le Verdon on the other hand - had been skirted, ignored, some of them to remain under the Nazi heel until the last day of the war (and **even the day after the armistice was signed in the case of the Channel Islands).** But the greater part of Belgium, all of Luxemburg, and almost all of France, excepting Alsace and Lorraine, had,

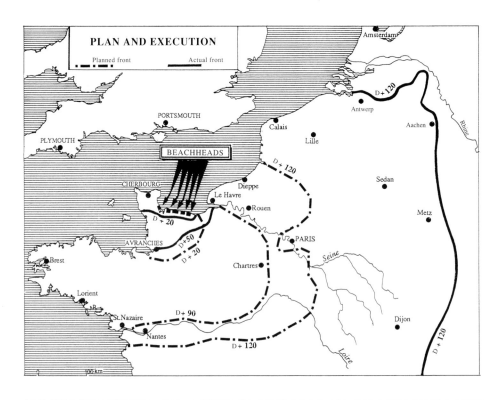

PLAN AND EXECUTION

Planned front — — — — Actual front ————

Amsterdam
Antwerp
Aachen
Rhine
PORTSMOUTH
Calais
Lille
PLYMOUTH
Sedan
BEACHHEADS
CHERBOURG
Dieppe
Le Havre
Rouen
Metz
D + 120
D + 120
D + 120
D + 20
PARIS
AVRANCHES
D + 50
D + 20
Seine
Brest
Chartres
Lorient
Dijon
St.Nazaire
D + 90
Nantes
D + 120
Loire
100 km

30

before the autumn, enjoyed prodigious advances on the date of the end of their sufferings: it is to the hasty withdrawal of German Seventh and Fifth Armies caught in the Mortain-Falaise trap, and by way of consequence, to the withdrawal of Fifteenth Army from the Pas-de-Calais and Nineteenth Army from Provence, not forgetting the link-up at Nod-sur-Seine enclosing the First Army of the Atlantic in a colossal prisoners' cage, that three countries could bring out the flags earlier that anticipated.

44 Allied divisions took part in the Battle of Normandy: 13 British, to which must be added the equivalent of 4 divisions in the form of 14 independent brigades including the two Green Beret brigades, the Belgian brigade, the Dutch brigade, the British SAS regiment and the two French SAS battalions; 3 Canadian divisions; the Polish armoured division; the three Canadian volunteer divisions; 22 American divisions; the Leclerc division.

With units that poured in during the autumn and those arriving from Provence and Italy, by 8th May 1945, the last day of the war in Europe, some 93 divisions, that is 4,581,000 men, supported by 1,335,000 airmen and ground crews, had come under the command of General Dwight David Eisenhower.

HOW THEY LANDED IN NORMANDY

	6th June	7th-14th June	15th-28th June	1st-15th July	16th-31st July	August
BRITISH	3rd Inf. 50th Inf. 51st Highl. 79th Arm'd 6th AB 49th Inf. 1 Commando Bde 4 Commando Bde	VII Army (8th) XI Army (13th) 15th Scottish (14th) 43rd Wessex (14th)	53rd Welsh (27th) 59th Staffs (27th) Guards (28 th)			
CANADIAN	3rd Inf.			2nd Inf. (7th)	4th Arm'd (31st)	
POLISH					1st Arm'd (31st)	
U.S.	82nd Airb. 101st Airb. 1st Inf. 4th Inf. elts 29th Inf. elts 90th Inf.	29th Inf. (7th) 90th Inf. (10th) 2nd Inf. (8th) 9th Inf. (14 th)	30th Inf. (15th) 79th Inf. (19th) 83rd Inf. (27th)	II Army (2nd) 8th Inf. (8th) III Army (9th) 35th Inf. (11th)	5th Inf. (16th) 28th Inf. (27th) IV Army (28th) VI Army (28th)	V Army (2nd) 80th Inf. (8th) VII Army (14th)
FRENCH						2nd Arm'd (1st)
BELGIAN						Brigade (7th)
DUTCH						Brigade (7th)
GRAND TOTAL	11	19	25	30	36	40

GERMAN REINFORCEMENTS ARRIVE

To the 11 infantry divisions and 3 parachute divisions - Seventh Army - present in Normandy on 6th June, and to the 3 tank divisions (21st Panzer, 2nd Panzer, 12th SS Panzer) immediately available, other units gradually joined that were brought in from elsewhere.

FROM	8th-15th June	16th-30th June	1st-15th July	16th-31st July	1st-15th August	16th-31st August
Fifteenth Army Pays de Caux Pas de Calais		346th Inf. (29th) 711st Inf (29th)		84th Inf. (30th) 326th Inf. (30th) 331st Inf. (30th)	48th Inf. (15th) 85th Inf. (5th) 17th Luftwaffe (15th)	49th Inf. (20th) 18th Luftwaffe (20th)
Nineteenth Army South-east France		277th Inf. (29th)		271st Inf. (24th) 272nd Inf. (24th)	338th Inf. (15th)	
First Atlantic Army		276th Inf. (29th)		708th Inf. (30th)		
Norway Denmark Holland	16th Luftwaffe			363rd Inf. (30th)	89th inf.	
Panzers	Lehr (8th) 17th SS (12th)	1st SS Pzer 2nd SS Pzer 9th SS (25th) 10th SS (25th)		116th Pzer (20th)	9th Pzer	

31

BY THE SAME AUTHOR

Collection "La Bataille de Normandie", Eds Presses de la Cité:
(*)   *STALINGRAD EN NORMANDIE*
(**)   *OPERATION PADDLE*
(***)   *LA RUCKMARSCH*
(****)   *MONTGOMERY CROSSES THE SEINE*
(*****) *LE HAVRE 44 A FEU ET A SANG*

LE NOUVEAU GUIDE DES CHAMPS DE BATAILLE DE NORMANDIE,
    50th anniversary edition, Eds Presses de la Cité

Published by Eds France Empire:
    TÉMOINS DE LA LIBÉRATION DE PARIS,
    in cooperation with Philippe Rageneau, Compagnon de la Libération
    LES BERETS VERTS FRANCAIS DU 6 JUIN
    a historical commentary on Philippe Kieffer's book

Published by Eds Montparnasse Multimédia & Mille Médias:
    D DAY : LES 100 JOURS DU 6 JUIN,
    the first CD Rom devoted to the battle of Normandy (in collaboration
    with Pierre Raiman, Louis Tanguy and Philippe Loranchet).

Published by Eds Hachette:
    GUIDE DU ROUTARD NORMANDIE JUBILÉE

Published by Tallandier-Historia
    LES 5 PLAGES DU 6 JUIN
    Itinerary guide
    THE FIVE D DAY BEACHES
    English version

Translations:
    LA NUIT DES CANONS DE MERVILLE
    John Golley, Presses de la Cité
    LES BERETS ROUGES S'ELANCENT EN NORMANDIE
    Sir Huw Wheldon, Comité du Débarquement

Foreign language translations;
    THE BATTLE OF THE FALAISE GAP
    Elek Pub, Londres
    THE BATTLE OF THE FALAISE GAP
    Ryerson Press, Ottawa
    THE BATTLE OF THE FALAISE GAP
    Hawthorn Pub, New York
    KOCIOL FALAISE
    M.O.N. Varsovie

Cover photograph: Jurques, 2nd August 1944.

Photographic credits. Public Archives of Canada, Bundesarchiv, Edimedia, IWM, Mémorial de Caen, Mémorial du Maréchal Leclerc de Hauteclocque et de la Libération de Paris and Musée Jean Moulin, PPP/IPS, USIS; Rights reserved: pages 3, 7 (1), 14, 19, 20, 28 (2).

© 1994 - Edilarge S.A. - Editions Ouest-France, Rennes - I.S.B.N. : 2.7373.1628.6
Dépôt légal : avril 1994 - N° d'éditeur : 3017.01.05.04.94
Imprimerie Raynard, La Guerche-de-Bretagne (35)